THE CORONATION OF KING CHARLES III
SECOND EDITION

History of the Ceremony and Traditions

THE CORONATION OF KING CHARLES III

HISTORY OF THE CEREMONY AND TRADITIONS

BY

DAVID I. WOOD

All rights reserved. No part of this book may be reproduced, stored in a retrieval system, or transmitted in any form or by any means, electronic, mechanical, photocopying, recording, or otherwise, without the prior written permission of the copyright holder.

This book is a work of nonfiction and is based on the author's research. While every effort has been made to ensure the accuracy of the information presented in this book, the publisher and the author assume no responsibility for errors or omissions.

INTRODUCTION

INTRODUCTION TO THE BRITISH CORONATION CEREMONY

The British coronation ceremony is a centuries-old tradition that marks the formal investiture of a new monarch as the head of state of the United Kingdom. The ceremony is steeped in symbolism and ritual, and it reflects the rich history and cultural traditions of the British monarchy.

The coronation ceremony typically takes place several months after the death or abdication of the previous monarch. It is a grand, public event that is attended by thousands of people, including dignitaries, government officials, and members of the general public. The ceremony is also televised and broadcast around the world, making it a significant moment in the global media landscape.

The coronation ceremony begins with the arrival of the new monarch at Westminster Abbey, the traditional site of coronations in England. The monarch is greeted by a procession of clergy, who lead the way into the abbey. The ceremony itself is conducted by the Archbishop of Canterbury, the spiritual leader of the Church of England, and it is attended by bishops and other religious leaders from a variety of denominations.

During the coronation ceremony, the new monarch is anointed with holy oil and crowned with the Imperial State Crown, which is one of the most important symbols of the British monarchy. The crown is made of gold and is encrusted with diamonds, pearls, and other precious stones. It is also adorned with a number of symbolic objects, such as the Black Prince's Ruby and the Koh-i-Noor diamond.

After the coronation, the new monarch delivers a speech in which they pledge to serve the people of the United Kingdom and to uphold the traditions and values of the monarchy. The ceremony also includes the singing of hymns and the reading of passages from the Bible. The ceremony has evolved over the centuries, but it is traditionally a grand and elaborate spectacle that involves many different elements, including religious rituals, music, and pageantry.

In addition to the coronation ceremony itself, there are a number of other events and traditions that are associated with the investiture of a new monarch. These include the State Opening of Parliament, which takes place shortly after the coronation, and the Trooping the Colour, which is an annual military parade that celebrates the birthday of the reigning monarch.

Overall, the British coronation ceremony is a deeply significant and symbolic event that reflects the rich history and cultural traditions of the United Kingdom. It is a momentous occasion that is celebrated by people around the world, and it serves as a reminder of the enduring role of the monarchy in British society.

CHAPTER 1

HISTORY OF THE BRITISH CORONATION CEREMONY

Traditional English coronations took place in Westminster Abbey, with the ruler occupying the Coronation Chair. The foundational components of the coronation service and the first kind of oath may be linked to the ritual Saint Dunstan created for Edgar's coronation at Bath Abbey in 973 AD. It took inspiration from the rituals employed by the Frankish rulers and the ordination of bishops. There are two pre-Norman Conquest types of coronation ceremonies called as ordines or recensions (from the Latin word ordo, which means "order"). Edgar in 973 and other Anglo-Saxon and early Norman rulers utilized the second recension; it is unknown whether the first recension was ever used in England.

A third recension, which was used in 1135 during the coronation of Henry I's successor, Stephen, was most likely written during the reign of Henry I. The Pontificale Romano-Germanicum, a book of German liturgy published in Mainz in 961, drew substantially from the consecration of the Holy Roman Emperor, keeping the most significant aspects of the Anglo-Saxon ritual but also bringing the English tradition in line with continental practice. It was in use until Edward II's coronation in 1308 when the fourth recension, which had been assembled over many decades before, was first used. The new ordo, however inspired by its French equivalent, placed a more emphasis on the oath and the balance between the monarch and his nobility than did the absolutist French rulers. The Liber Regalis in Westminster Abbey, one manuscript of this recension, is now thought to represent the final form.

The young king Edward VI was crowned at the first Protestant coronation in England after the commencement of the reformation in 1547, when Archbishop Thomas Cranmer delivered a sermon denouncing paganism and "the tyranny of the bishops of Rome." Six years later, Mary I, his half-sister, succeeded him and brought back the Catholic rite. Elizabeth I was crowned in England for the last time under the authority of the Catholic Church in 1559, although Owen Oglethorpe, a low-ranking bishop of Carlisle, presided over the ceremony because Elizabeth insisted on modifications to reflect her Protestant convictions.

Modern coronation

For the coronation of James I in 1603, the Liber Regalis was translated into English for the first time, partly in response to the reformation in England, which demanded that services be understood by the populace, but also in an effort by antiquarians to reclaim a lost English identity from before the Norman Conquest. James II, a Catholic, authorized a condensed form of the liturgy in 1685 that left out the Eucharist, but following kings reinstated it. Henry Compton rewrote the liturgy once again for the coronations of William III and Mary II only four years later. Because Latin was the sole language shared by the German-speaking George I and the clergy, it was revived at his coronation in 1714. The second time around, spectacle eclipsed the religious component of the event, perhaps as a result of the "many blunders and stupidities" that plagued George III's coronation in 1761. George IV's coronation in 1821 was a pricey and opulent event that cost a significant sum of money.

William IV, George's brother and successor, had to be convinced to be crowned at all; his ceremony, held in 1831 during a financial crisis, barely cost one-sixth of what had been spent on the previous occasion. The "Half Crown-nation" was threatened with a boycott by traditionalists. The monarch simply covered his uniform as Admiral of the Fleet with his robes. A variety of cost-cutting decisions were taken during this coronation that would become the standard for future kings and queens. The ceremony in Westminster Hall when peers would gather and present the monarch with regalia was dropped. A state carriage procession from St. James's Palace to the abbey was started in place of the foot March from Westminster Hall to the Abbey, and this pageantry is a significant aspect of the contemporary celebration. Following the formal ritual, the coronation dinner was also over.

When Victoria was crowned in 1838, the ceremony adhered to the condensed model established by her uncle, and the poorly prepared ceremony was marked by errors and mishaps. The big choir and orchestra were poorly coordinated, and just one new piece had been produced for the abbey's music, which received harsh criticism in the press.

With the coronation of Richard II in 1377, a 10-year-old child who was deemed unlikely to command respect just by his physical appearance, the notion that a new monarch needed to win the allegiance of the populace by making the process a show for the people first emerged. The lord mayor, aldermen, and livery companies greeted the young king and his entourage outside the City of London the day before the coronation, and they led him to the London Tower where he spent the night in vigil. The king rode in a large procession through the festively lit city streets to Westminster the next morning. A replica palace had been erected in Cheapside, likely to stand in for the New Jerusalem, where a girl blew gold leaf over the king and gave him drink. Bands performed along the path, and the public conduits were flowing with red and white wine. Similar or even more extravagant pageants persisted until Charles II's coronation in 1661.

Early modern coronations were often documented by artists who then released lavish folio volumes of engravings portraying the proceedings within the monastery. The last of these was published in 1905 and showed the coronation that had occurred three years previously. Reenactments of the ceremony were performed in theaters in London and rural areas; in 1761, a play at the Royal Opera House in Covent Garden that featured the Westminster Abbey choir lasted for three months after the actual event.

It wasn't until 1902 that the necessity of including the various facets of the British Empire in coronations was put into consideration. Those in attendance included the prime ministers and governors general of the by that point nearly fully autonomous British Dominions, as well as a significant number of the leaders of the Indian Princely States and the various British Protectorates. A further Imperial Conference was convened. Along with the customary banners of the Home Nations, the procession inside Westminster Abbey in 1911 included the flags of the dominions and the Indian Empire. By 1937, the dominions had achieved complete independence via the Statute of Westminster 1931, and the language of the coronation oath had been changed to include their names and restrict the provisions pertaining to religion to the United Kingdom.

Thus, since 1937, the king has been crowned as the ruler of numerous other independent countries in addition to the United Kingdom, collectively known as the Commonwealth realms since 1953.

Timing of Coronation

Throughout British history, the coronation's date has changed. The coronation of King Edgar took place around 15 years after his accession in 957 and may have been held to commemorate the pinnacle of his rule or his 30th birthday. William I, the first Norman king, was also crowned on the day he became king, 25 December 1066, but three weeks after the surrender of English nobles and bishops at Berkhampstead, allowing time to prepare an impressive ceremony. Harold II was crowned the day after the death of his predecessor, Edward the Confessor, the rush likely reflecting the contentious nature of Harold's succession. Within a few weeks or even days after taking office, the majority of his successors were crowned. When Edward I took the throne in 1272, he was participating in the Ninth Crusade; he was crowned shortly after his return in 1274. A campaign in Scotland in 1307 similarly prevented Edward II from being crowned. When Henry VI became king in 1422, he was only a few months old. He was crowned in 1429 but did not legally take up the throne until 1437, when he was declared mature enough. The Christian Sabbath, a Sunday, or a Christian festival were the most common days for premodern coronations. Edgar was installed as king on Pentecost, William I was installed as king on Christmas Day, probably to emulate the Byzantine emperors, and John was installed on Ascension Day. Elizabeth I contacted John Dee, her astrologer, before selecting a lucky date. Charles II was crowned in 1661, and Anne was crowned in 1702, on St. George's Day, the celebration of England's patron saint.

The waiting period was extended to several months under the Hanoverian kings in the late eighteenth and early nineteenth centuries, after a period of mourning for the preceding monarch and to enable time for ritual preparation. Every king between George IV and George V had a minimum of a 12-month interval between their accession and coronation. George VI, who succeeded Edward VIII and was crowned five months after the latter's ascension, was not crowned. The date for his predecessor's coronation had already been determined; with a new king, preparations merely resumed.

The coronations of the Anglo-Saxon kings took place in a variety of places, including as Bath, Kingston upon Thames, London, and Winchester. The Westminster Abbey served as the site of all subsequent coronations after Harold II, the last Anglo-Saxon king, was installed there in 1066. Henry III was crowned in 1216 in Gloucester when rebels controlled London. He subsequently decided to conduct asecond coronation in 1220 at Westminster. Henry VI was crowned as king of England in London in 1429 and as king of France in Paris two centuries later.

CHAPTER 2

ROLE OF THE ARCHBISHOP OF CANTERBURY IN THE CORONATION CEREMONY

St. Augustine served as the first Archbishop of Canterbury. Pope Gregory I had sent him on a mission to the English, and he landed in Kent in 597 CE. In or around the year 598, he converted to Christianity and was welcomed by King Ethelbert. It seems that Pope Gregory had planned for the new archepiscopal sees for England to be constructed in London and York but was unaware of previous events in the ancient Roman province, particularly the growth of the Pelagian heresy. Due to political reasons, Canterbury was ultimately selected instead of London. Since that time, the Canterbury Archbishops have been referred to as sitting in St. Augustine's chair.

The Church of England was an essential element of the continental Western European Church prior to the rupture with papal authority in the sixteenth century. Despite no longer being in communion with the See of Rome, the Church of England, a well-established national church, continues to see itself as a part of the larger Western Catholic heritage and as the "mother church" of the Anglican Communion worldwide.

The selection of the Archbishop of Canterbury and other bishops varied greatly over the Middle Ages. The King of

England, the Pope, and the Canterbury Cathedral canons have all made the decision at different points in history. Since the English Reformation, the Church of England has been more overtly a state church, and now the Prime Minister makes the decision on behalf of the Sovereign from a shortlist of two candidates chosen by an ad hoc commission known as the Crown Nominations Commission. Archbishops in the past have served the country and the Church with distinction. They eagerly embraced ecumenism and interreligious dialogue in the second half of the 20th century, assisting the church and the country in adjusting to the reality of a society that was becoming more and more pluralistic. Some view the Archbishop's automatic leadership of the global Anglican Communion as a vestige of colonialism and call into doubt his authority. The function of the Archbishop would alter if the Church of England were disestablished. Future archbishops are likely to continue to speak out in favor of working with others to create a better world, regardless of their political affiliation, given the excellent caliber of people nominated to this position.

The archbishop performs four key functions:

The east of the County of Kent is covered by the Diocese of Canterbury, whose diocesan bishop he is. It is the earliest see in the English church and was established in 597.

He serves as the metropolitan archbishop of Canterbury, a province that includes the southern two-thirds of England.

He serves as the senior primate and head of the Church of England in his capacity as Primate of All England (the British sovereign is the "Supreme governor" of the church). Along with his colleague, the Archbishop of York, he serves on or leads many of the church's significant boards and committees. However, since the church lacks a strong center of authority, the two archbishops often have to lead by persuasion. Due to his prominent public position and involvement in important national events like the British monarch's coronation, the news media often seeks out the Archbishop of Canterbury's comments.

Although the archbishop has no legal standing outside of England, he or she is regarded by custom as primus inter pares ("first among equals") among all Anglican primates across the globe. The Lambeth Conferences, which he has organized about every ten years since 1867, bring together Anglican bishops from all around the globe. The larger Anglican communion, however, has no influence on the choice of a new archbishop.

He represents Anglicans in England and across the globe in the final two of these roles, playing a significant ecumenical and interfaith role.

The coronation of the British monarch has a major role for the Archbishop of Canterbury. The official succession of a new monarch to the throne is marked by the coronation ceremony, a customary and symbolic event.

The administration of the coronation oath and the anointing of the new king are under the direction of the Archbishop of Canterbury during the ritual. The coronation oath is a solemn pledge made by the ruler to defend the Christian religion and rule in accordance with the legislation of the kingdom. The king is anointed with holy oil during the anointing, a symbolic ceremony that represents the divine power and consecration of the monarch's position as head of the Church of England.

During the event, the Archbishop also preaches. Typically, this sermon touches on the monarch's obligations and duties, the value of religion, and the place of the Church in society.

The Archbishop of Canterbury additionally has a variety of other obligations in regard to the coronation ceremony in addition to these. These include managing the ceremony's planning, liaising with other religious leaders and government representatives, and representing the Church of England during the coronation.

During the procession of the clergy and other dignitaries before the entry of the sovereign, the litany of the saints is chanted. I was happy, a song from Psalm 122, is sung to mark the monarch's entry.

The royal sits on a Chair of Estate when they enter Westminster Abbey wearing the red surcoat and the Robe of State made of crimson velvet.

East, south, west, and north of the coronation theater are the Garter Principal King of Arms, the Archbishop of Canterbury, the Lord Chancellor, the Lord Great Chamberlain, the Lord High Constable, and the Earl Marshal.

The archbishop requests that the sovereign be acknowledged from each side, saying:

"Sirs, allow me to introduce to you [name], your undisputed King or Queen.

Therefore, are those of you who have come on this day to pay your respects and provide service prepared to do likewise?"

The archbishop then gives the sovereign an oath after the people have proclaimed the sovereign on each side. The Coronation Oath Act of 1688 mandated that the sovereign "Promise and Swear to Govern the People of this Kingdom of England and the Dominions thereto pertaining according to the Statues in Parliament Agreed on and the Laws and Customs of the same" after the Glorious Revolution.

A prayer based on the historic Deus electorum fortitudo, which is also used in the anointing of French monarchs, is said by the Archbishop before the anointing.

Following this prayer, the choir sings the coronation hymn Zadok the Priest by George Frederick Handel. In the meanwhile, the monarch removes the crimson robe and walks in the anointing gown to the Coronation Chair, which has been placed prominently.

Overall, the role of the Archbishop of Canterbury in the coronation ceremony is to provide spiritual guidance and direction to the new monarch, and to help consecrate and sanctify the new monarch's role as head of the Church of England and the United Kingdom.

CHAPTER 3

THE CORONATION OATH AND ITS SIGNIFICANCE

The Second Recension, which was used in 973 for King Edgar, provided the overall foundation for the coronation rite. The order of swearing an oath, anointing, investing in regalia, crowning, and enthronement contained in the Anglo-Saxon text hasn't changed despite the service going through two significant changes, a translation, and being altered for each coronation over the next thousand years. Holy Communion serves as the backdrop for the coronation rituals.

The royal sits on a Chair of Estate when they enter Westminster Abbey wearing the red surcoat and the Robe of State made of crimson velvet. East, south, west, and north of the coronation theater are the Garter Principal King of Arms, the Archbishop of Canterbury, the Lord Chancellor, the Lord Great Chamberlain, the Lord High Constable, and the Earl Marshal.

The monarch may also take the Accession Declaration, if they haven't already, in addition to the oath. The Bill of Rights of 1689 established the precedent for this proclamation, which must be made either during the crowning of a new monarch or at the first session of parliament after their accession (also known as the State Opening of Parliament). Prior to the coronation, the monarch also takes a second pledge to uphold Presbyterian church administration in the Church of Scotland.

Following the swearing-in, an ecclesiastic hands the ruler a Bible and declares, "Here is Wisdom; This is the regal Law; These are the alive Oracles of God." The Apocrypha and the whole King James Version of the Bible are utilized. The Moderator of the General Assembly of the Church of Scotland gave Elizabeth II the Bible during her coronation. Following the reading of the Bible, there is Holy Communion with a special collection for the coronation. However, the service was cut short after the Nicene Creed. At Elizabeth II's coronation, the gospel reading was Matthew 22:15–22, which includes Jesus's well-known command to "give unto Caesar the things that are Caesar's" and the epistle reading was 1

Peter 2:13–17, which urges readers to respect and obey governmental authorities.

CORONATION OATH SIGNIFICANCE

During the coronation ceremony, a sovereign makes a formal declaration in which they pledge to maintain the laws and traditions of their kingdom or empire and to honorably serve their people. This declaration is known as the coronation oath. Depending on the nation and the particular traditions of the monarchy, the oath's precise language varies, but it often contains a dedication to justice, compassion, and the advancement of the common good.

The coronation oath's roots may be found in the ancient world, when kings and queens were often forced to make a serious pledge to the gods or to the populace as a method to show their dedication to preserving the law and safeguarding their subjects. The coronation oath assumed a more formal form in medieval Europe, when the king vowed to uphold the privileges and rights of the nobles, the church, and the common people.

The oath made by English and British monarchs, which has altered over time but generally stayed identical since Queen Victoria's coronation in 1838, is one of the most well-known instances of a coronation oath. The following clauses are included in the current English coronation oath, which is administered by the Archbishop of Canterbury:

The king pledges to uphold both the "professed faith of the Church of England" and the laws of God.

The king or queen swears to uphold the nation's laws and traditions and to rule the populace "in accordance with the same."

In keeping with English law, the king swears to "preserve inevitably the settlement of the Church of England, and the doctrine, worship, discipline, and governance thereof."

"Defend and maintain the rights and privileges of the Church of England, as well as the rights and privileges of the bishops and clergy of the Church, and to preserve to the bishops and clergy of the Church, and to all the churches of the realm, the liberties, franchises, and immunities granted to them by law," the monarch pledges.

The coronation oath is a significant representation of the monarch's dedication to upholding the law and safeguarding the rights and liberties of the populace. It serves as a reminder of the monarch's duties as head of state and the part they play in upholding the country's stability and unity.

The coronation oath has a functional function in addition to its ceremonial one. The monarch swears to preserve the nation's laws and traditions and to serve the populace honorably by taking the oath. The king will be more likely to behave honorably and in the best interests of the country as a result, as opposed to advancing their own personal or political goals.

In many nations across the globe, the coronation oath is a revered custom that has contributed significantly to the history and development of monarchy and constitutional governance. The coronation oath serves as a reminder of the duties and responsibilities associated with the position of head of state, as well as the significance of respecting the law and honorably serving the people, whether it is taken by a king or queen, an emperor or empress, or any other form of monarch.

Chapter 4

BRIEF BIOGRAPHY OF KING CHARLES III

On November 14, 1948, Charles was born, and King George VI was his maternal grandpa. First child born to Philip, Duke of Edinburgh, and Princess Elizabeth, Duchess of Edinburgh (later Queen Elizabeth II). Three more children, Anne (born 1950), Andrew (born 1960), and Edward, were born to his parents (born 1964). Baptized by the Archbishop of Canterbury, Geoffrey Fisher, in the Music Room of Buckingham Palace when he was four weeks old.

Charles became the heir apparent when his grandpa passed away and his mother was crowned Queen Elizabeth II. As the king's oldest son and in accordance with a charter issued by King Edward III in 1337, he was automatically given the titles of Duke of Cornwall. Charles was present at Westminster Abbey during his mother's coronation.

A governess named Catherine Peebles was chosen to handle Charles' education at Buckingham Palace when he turned five. He was the first heir apparent to get his education from a public school rather than a private tutor. Stuart Townend, the school's founder and principal, suggested the Queen to have Charles train in football since the lads never showed any sign of deference to anybody on the football field, thus he did not get any special treatment. Then, starting in 1958, Charles attended two of his father's previous schools: Gordonstoun in Scotland's northeast, where he started lessons, and Cheam Preparatory School in Hampshire, England.

On July 26, 1958, Charles was appointed Prince of Wales and Earl of Chester, but his investiture was not conducted until July 1, 1969, when his mother gave him a televised coronation at Caernarfon Castle. The first monarch to address the House of Lords since the future Edward VII in 1884, he assumed his seat and delivered his first speech in June 1974. Charles started to take on additional official responsibilities; he established the Prince's Trust in 1976 and visited the US in 1981. In the middle of the 1970s, Australian Prime Minister Malcolm Fraser suggested that Charles run for Governor-General of Australia. Charles indicated interest in the position, but the plan failed due to a lack of support from the general people.

Following in the traditions of his father, grandfather, and two great-grandfathers, Charles served in both the Royal Air Force and the Royal Navy. He sought and obtained Royal Air Force training during his second year at Cambridge, learning to fly the Chipmunk with Cambridge University Air Squadron. To get his jet pilot training, he flew by himself to the Royal Air Force College Cranwell. In August 1971, he received his RAF wings. He began his naval career and enrolled in a six-week course at the Royal Naval

College Dartmouth after the passing-out parade in September.

Charles wed Lady Diana Frances Spencer, the 8th Earl Spencer's daughter, on July 29, 1981. She assumed the title of princess of Wales after the royal wedding, a major worldwide media event that was aired live on television and seen by hundreds of millions of people. Prince William of Wales, the couple's first child, was placed second in line for the throne at birth. On September 15, 1984, Prince Henry Charles Albert David, sometimes known as Harry, was born.

As a result of intensive media scrutiny and adultery rumors, Charles and Diana's marriage progressively became strained. Charles and Diana made the decision to divorce on December 9, 1992, although they would still carry out their public responsibilities and co-parent their boys. The divorce was finalized on August 28, 1996. The conventional kind of monarchy that Charles stood for was put in jeopardy when Diana died in a car accident a year later. Public sentiment for her was much greater in death than it was in life. He then put a lot of work into updating his public persona as the heir apparent. He wed Camilla Parker Bowles, with whom he had a protracted romance, on April 9, 2005.

Charles announced his engagement to Camilla Parker Bowles, and he gave her a ring that belonged to his grandmother, Queen Elizabeth the Queen Mother. In a Privy Council meeting, the Queen signed off on the marriage. The Queen's Privy

Council for Canada did not need to convene in order to approve the marriage, according to the Canadian Department of Justice, since the relationship would not produce children and would not affect the succession to the throne of Canada.

Charles served as the Queen's representative in formal capacities when he was the Prince of Wales. He presided over investitures and went to foreign dignitaries' funerals. Charles often visited Wales, taking part in a week's worth of engagements every summer, and attending significant national events like the Senedd's opening. Under his presidency, the Royal Collection Trust's six trustees convened three times a year.

In order to promote Welsh talent for the harp, the native instrument of Wales,

Charles reinstated the custom of the Prince of Wales having an official harpist. His involvement in the Canadian Armed Forces enables him to follow soldier operations, visit them whether they are in Canada or abroad, and take part in ceremonial events.

After his mother, Queen Elizabeth II, passed away on September 8, 2022, Charles succeeded to the throne of Great Britain. After surpassing Edward VII's record of 59 years on April 20, 2011, Charles was the British heir apparent with the longest reign. He was the oldest person to become a monarch at the age of 73; the previous record-holder was William IV, who was 64 when he became king in 1830.

The King's desire for the event to reflect the ethnic mix of contemporary Britain calls for it to be shorter, smaller, less costly, and more inclusive of many religions and community organizations. Even so, the coronation will be a Church of England ritual that calls for the administration of the coronation oath, anointing, delivery of the orb, and enthronement.

CHAPTER 5

CORONATION OF CHARLES III AND CAMILLA

After Queen Elizabeth II passed away on September 8, her son Charles, the former Prince of Wales, instantly took over as the country's new king. The British royal family stated today that Charles will be formally crowned on May 7, 2023, despite the fact that he has already formally adopted the title King Charles III.

King Charles III had a selection of monikers. Charles Philip Arthur George Windsor is his complete name, yet he had the option of choosing any of his four given names. Camilla Parker Bowles, his spouse, is now the queen consort.

The complex legal processes that must be followed whilst a British monarch is still in power are spelled out in full by British traditions, as are the prerequisites for gaining the throne.

It has already taken place. Prince Charles is no longer a prince since he is now the monarch of the United Kingdom because Queen Elizabeth passed away.

Following the death of the outgoing monarch, the British constitution stipulates that the successor to the throne instantly assumes the role of king or queen. There is no interregnum, which is a time when neither a queen nor a king is in power.

Charles' time will be mostly consumed with the formal procedures for taking the throne until May, however. King Charles III was proclaimed the next monarch of Britain by the Accession Council, which convened at St. James' Palace on September 10, 2022, two days after Queen Elizabeth II passed away. The two-part Privy Council meeting was the new king's first formal ceremony, during which he took an oath to uphold the Church of Scotland.

King Charles III began his meeting tour after the council's pronouncement by convening talks with the new British Prime Minister and the cabinet, the head of the opposition party, the Archbishop of Canterbury (Justin Welby), and the Dean of Westminster.

Then followed the obligatory journey to Wales and Northern Ireland, where he met with top ministers and accepted condolences. England, Scotland, Northern Ireland, and Wales form the United Kingdom of Great Britain and Northern Ireland, or the UK.

King Charles will collaborate with the "Operation Golden Orb" group to organize the ceremony from now until the coronation. The most recent coronation in Britain drew 8,000 spectators and lasted more than three hours.

The inauguration of King Charles will take place on May 7, 2023. The crowning of the British monarch is mostly a ceremonial event. There is no issue with the monarchy being vacant since King

Charles ascended to the throne immediately after Queen Elizabeth II passed away.

On June 2, 1953, some 16 months after the death of her father, King George VI, on February 6, 1952, Queen Elizabeth II was formally crowned.

Since 1066, the Archbishop of Canterbury has presided over all royal coronation rituals, which have been held in Westminster Abbey for the last 900 years. King Charles will make a promise to "reign according to law, to apply justice with compassion, and to sustain the Church of England" at the event. He will accept the orb and scepter of the Crown Jewels and the Archbishop's benediction. King Charles will then have a crown placed on his head by the Archbishop. King Charles III is not permitted to don any of the several crowns housed in the British Crown Jewels prior to his coronation.

As Earl Marshal, the Duke of Norfolk is often in charge of planning the occasion. Edward Fitzalan-Howard, the 18th Duke, is the current earl marshal. The coronation will be organized by a committee of privy counselors.

The coronation of Charles and Camilla will take place on Saturday, May 6, 2023, at Westminster Abbey, it was revealed in October 2022. The date was chosen by Buckingham Palace to give people time to grieve Queen Elizabeth II's passing before a festive event. The government announced an additional bank holiday on

May 8, 2023 two days after the coronation in November 2022.

Statutory requirements for a coronation oath, anointing, orb delivery, and enthronement must all be followed. The King will be crowned using St. Edward's Crown, which was taken out of the Tower of London in December 2022 to be resized. Throughout the event, the King will also don the Imperial State Crown. The Stone of Scone will be transported from the Crown Room of Edinburgh Castle to London for Charles's coronation at Westminster Abbey and then returned to the Castle after the event, according to a September 2022 announcement by Historic Environment Scotland.

Camilla, Charles' wife, will also be anointed as queen consort at the same time as him. Clarence House proclaimed that Camilla would not become queen after Charles' ascension when he married her in 2005. Elizabeth II expressed her "sincere hope" that Camilla be recognized as queen consort upon Charles's ascension in February 2022, since Camilla's popularity was increasing at the time. Charles, however, had long intended for her to be so named and crowned with him. Since the 1937 coronation of his grandmother Queen Elizabeth (after known as the Queen Mother), this will be the first time a consort has assumed the throne.

The British government covers the cost of the coronation since it is a state event.

The British royal family, the British prime minister, legislators from both chambers of Parliament, as well as foreign heads of state and royalty, will all be on the guest list, which is also decided by the government. Charles and Camilla are anticipated to arrive on the Buckingham Palace balcony after the ceremony.

There are typically six stages to the coronation:

The recognition: The Archbishop of Canterbury will introduce the monarch to those assembled in the Abbey while standing next to the Coronation Chair. "God Save the King!" will be yelled by the assembly as trumpets blast.

The pledge: Following that, the ruler takes an oath to support the law and the Church of England.

The anointing: The King will sit on the Coronation Chair after taking off his ceremonial robe. To hide the King from view, a gold-cloth canopy will be held over the chair. With holy oil prepared according to a secret mixture that is believed to include ambergris, orange blossoms, roses, jasmine, and cinnamon, the Archbishop will anoint the King's hands, breast, and head.

The investiture: The Sovereign's Sceptre, a gold rod topped with a white enameled dove, a symbol of justice and compassion, will then be delivered to the sovereign when she returns to the Coronation Chair, together with the Royal Orb, the Sceptre, and other artifacts. The King will then receive St. Edward's Crown from the Archbishop.

Enthronement and Homage: The King will rise to the throne from the coronation chair. Then, peers would bow before the ruler in respect.

Then the Queen Consort will be crowned and anointed in the same manner.

CHAPTER 6

THE ROYAL REGALIA (CROWN JEWELS)

Archaeologists discovered the 1st known usage of a crown in Britain at Deal, Kent, in 1988. It dates to about 200 and 150 BCE. The Mill Hill Warrior's tomb included a sword, a brooch, a ceremonial shield, and a beautiful bronze crown with a single arch that rested squarely on the wearer's head. Crowns were worn during this time by military and religious leaders as emblems of power. Following the Roman invasion of Britain in 43 CE, priests kept using crowns.

When England turned to Christianity in the Early Middle Ages, rulers there began wearing regalia. After Edward the Confessor was canonized in the 12th century, a permanent set of coronation regalia was created in his honor. Another set of regalia was saved for religious feasts and State Openings of Parliament, and these sacred relics were maintained at Westminster Abbey, the site of coronations since 1066. These items together became known as the Jewels of the Crown. The majority of the current collection was created roughly 350 years ago, just after Charles II came to power. After the monarchy was overthrown in 1649 during the English Civil War, the medieval and Tudor regalia had been sold or destroyed. A late 12th-century anointing spoon, which is the oldest piece, and three early 17th-century swords are the only original objects that predate the Restoration. Following the union of the kingdoms of England and Scotland in 1707, the regalia was still worn by British kings.

Crown exchanges served as a symbol of the passing of power between kings. The Welsh regalia, including the fabled King Arthur's crown, were given to England when Edward I (1272–1307) defeated the Welsh prince Llewelyn ap Gruffydd in 1282. The rulers of England received the glory of Wales and the Welsh people. The Stone of Scone was transported to the Tower of London in commemoration of a kingdom's capitulation and conquest during the invasion of Scotland in 1296, according to the historian Walter of Guisborough. It was placed inside a wooden chair that eventually became known as the Coronation Chair since it was used for the investiture of monarchs of England. Scotland finally recovered her freedom, and the Scottish regalia were also brought to London and presented to Edward the Confessor's mausoleum. There were ten crowns in all in Edward II's (1307–1327) treasury. When Richard II (1377–1399) was compelled to resign, he said, "I present and offer to you this crown... and all the powers depending on it," symbolically transferring the St. Edward's Crown to his successor.

The king is clothed in clothes and jewels, anointed with holy oil from an ampulla poured into the spoon, and crowned with St. Edward's Crown during a coronation. The lighter Imperial State Crown is then substituted, which is also often worn for State Openings of Parliament. A simpler set of regalia is given to royal wives, and since 1831, a unique crown has been created for each queen consort. State swords, trumpets, ceremonial maces, church plate, historical regalia, banqueting plate, and royal baptism fonts are also recognized as crown treasures. They are a part of the Royal Collection and are handed down from one king to the next as part of the institution of monarchy. The Jewels are kept out in the open at the Martin Tower and Jewel House, where they are seen by 2.5 million people annually while not in use.

After the Restoration, the State Crown of Mary of Modena, wife of James II, who first wore it during their coronation in

1685, was customarily worn by kings-queens consort. A similar diadem that consorts wore in procession to the Abbey is now set with crystals and cultured pearls in place of the original 561 rented diamonds and 129 pearls. It is on display at the Jewel House. 177 diamonds, 1 ruby, 1 sapphire, and 1 emerald were previously set in the diadem. That crown was seen to be overly theatrical and in need of repair by the 19th century, so in 1831 Queen Adelaide, the wife of William IV, had the Crown of Queen Adelaide constructed using diamonds from her own jewelry.

The Crown of Queen Elizabeth was made for Queen Elizabeth, the wife of George VI and afterwards known as the Queen Mother, to wear during their coronation since Mary continued to wear the crown (without its arches) after George V's death. It is the first British crown constructed completely of platinum, and while it has four instead of eight half-arches, Queen Mary's Crown served as its inspiration. About 2,800 diamonds total, including the Koh-i-Noor in the center of the front cross, are used in the crown's decoration. It also includes a duplicate of the 22.5-carat Lahore Diamond that the East India Company gave to Queen Victoria in 1851 as well as a 17.3-carat diamond that Abdülmecid I, Sultan of the Ottoman Empire, gave her in 1856. In 2002, during the Queen Mother's laying in state and burial, the crown was placed on top of her casket.

DRESS

Several attendees of the event don unique robes, uniforms, or costumes. Prior to each Coronation, the Earl Marshal issues a detailed dress code for attendees (apart from members of the royal family) that is published in the London Gazette.

Throughout the event, the sovereign dons a number of robes and various outfits. Contrary to the regalia's history and tradition, most coronation gowns are typically produced from scratch for each king. (The supertunica and Robe Royal, which both originate from George IV's coronation in 1821, are the current exceptions.)

worn during the procession and the first half of the service:

Under all other garments, the crimson surcoat serves as the standard attire for the majority of the ritual. Elizabeth II dispensed with the surcoat in 1953 and wore a custom-made gown.

Robe of State, made of red velvet: The first robe worn during a coronation was the Parliament Robe, which was afterwards worn for State Openings of Parliament. It has an ermine cape and a lengthy train made of red velvet that is laced with gold lace and more ermine.

Worn over the surcoat for the Anointing:

An austere and straightforward dress used during anointing. It has no decorations, is basic white, and fastens at the back.

Wearable for the parade that follows the closing portion of the service:

The purple surcoat, which is worn at the ceremony's conclusion, is its counterpart, the crimson surcoat.

Purple velvet imperial robe: worn at the end of the ritual as one leaves the monastery. It consists of a purple silk velvet cape with embroidered ermine trim that is entirely lined with English satin made of pure silk and has a train that is accented with Canadian ermine. Purple is reminiscent of the royal robes worn by Roman emperors.

Queens consort (including dowagers) and British princesses stand out among the rest of the royal family because they invariably cover their court clothes with purple velvet mantles that have ermine trim. The attire of the other royal family members present follows the rules outlined, with the exception that royal dukes don a special kind of peer's robe that contains six rows of ermine on the cape and more ermine on the miniver edging to the front of the robe.

THE CORONATION BANQUET

In the past, a feast was hosted in Westminster Hall in the Palace of Westminster just after the coronation (which is also the home to the Houses of Parliament). The Earl Marshal would ride to his left and the Lord High Constable would ride to his right as the King or Queen's Champion, a position held by the Dymoke family in connection with the Manor of Scrivelsby, rode into the hall on horseback while wearing knightly armor. The champion would then declare that he was prepared to battle anybody who denied the king in a proclamation made by a herald.

The process would then be repeated in the hall's center and at the High Table after the King's Champion had thrown down the challenge (where the sovereign would be seated). The royal would then offer a gold cup to the winner, who would then sip from it. This custom was omitted from Queen Victoria's coronation and was never reinstated. The coronation meal also included the Chief Butler of England, Grand Carver of England, and Master Carver of Scotland.

Since George IV's coronation in 1821, Westminster Hall has not hosted any banquets. His coronation was the most lavish in history; nevertheless, William IV, his brother and successor, did away with the meal out of economic need, breaking a 632-year-old tradition. A Coronation Fleet Review has also been staged annually since 1901. A crowning honors list is also made public prior to the coronation as a way to recognize the occasion.

Made in United States
North Haven, CT
21 May 2023